To:

From:

Message:

Published by Christian Art Publishers
PO Box 1599, Vereeniging, 1930, RSA

First edition 2024

Designed by Christian Art Publishers

Cover designed by Christian Art Publishers
Images used under license from Shutterstock.com

Printed in Vietnam

ISBN 978-1-77637-158-7 (Faux Leather)
ISBN 978-0-638-00245-4 (Hardcover)

24 25 26 27 28 29 30 31 32 33 – 10 9 8 7 6 5 4 3 2 1

101 Prayers to Cope with Depression

JOANNA TEIGEN

CHRISTIAN ART PUBLISHERS

Hear my prayer, O LORD;
listen to my plea!
Answer me because
You are faithful and *righteous*.
Come quickly, LORD,
and answer me,
for my depression deepens.
Don't turn away from me,
or I will die.
Let me hear of
Your *unfailing love*
each morning,
for I am trusting You.

Rescue me from
my enemies, LORD;
I run to You to hide me.
Teach me to do *Your will*,
for You are my God.
May Your *gracious Spirit*
lead me forward
on a firm footing.
For the *glory* of Your name,
O LORD, preserve my life.
Because of *Your faithfulness*,
bring me out of this distress.

Psalm 143:1, 7-11 NLT

"*Do not be afraid*
or discouraged,
for the LORD
will *personally*
go ahead of you.
He will *be with you;*
He will *neither fail you*
nor abandon you."

Deuteronomy 31:8 NLT

1

Light in the Darkness

If I say, "Surely the darkness will hide me
and the light become night around me,"
even the darkness will not be dark to You...
Psalm 139:11-12

Lord,

No matter which way I turn, all I can see is pain. Grief and frustration consume my emotions, while laughter and joy seem like a distant memory. I'm afraid I will sink so low or suffer so deeply that I'll never recover. I wonder if my struggles will leave me broken and alone.

You—and You only—are my light in this darkness. Nothing I feel is a secret to You. No problem is too great for You to solve, and nothing can hide me from Your eyes. I'm trusting You to search for me, find me, and carry me to a "spacious place" of safety and peace (2 Samuel 22:20). Because of Your love, I will be well.

Amen.

2

Seen and Known

She gave this name to the LORD who
spoke to her: "You are the God who sees me,"
for she said, "I have now seen the One who sees me."
Genesis 16:13

Lord,

I've learned to put on a brave face that hides the frightened and weary child inside. No one knows the pain of my unhealed wounds, anxieties, or shame. I feel invisible to everyone as I struggle to hold myself together. I wonder, *Who would listen if I raised my voice to cry for help?*

Yet You, Lord, discern the fake smiles that mask my tears. When I can't articulate my needs or emotions, You "perceive my thoughts from afar" (Psalm 139:2). As Your child, You know me better than I know myself. Thank You for never letting me out of Your sight. Teach me to rest in the comfort of Your presence and trust in Your love.

Amen.

3

The Peace of God

When I said, "My foot is slipping,"
Your unfailing love, LORD, supported
me. When anxiety was great within me,
Your consolation brought me joy.

Psalm 94:18-19

Lord,

You know the triggers that spike panic without warning. My heart pounds and it's hard to breathe. Racing thoughts make it impossible to think clearly or solve the issue at hand. As fear takes hold, I feel like lashing out, bursting into tears, or running for cover. It seems impossible to restore my sense of peace.

Yet You, Lord, are ready to meet me in the moment. Teach me to focus on Your Word that promises Your constant presence, power, and love. Move me to pray since You hear me when I cry out to You in distress (Psalm 55:17). Bear the Spirit's fruit of peace in my heart so I stand firm in the face of trouble. You are my comfort and joy.

Amen.

4

Jesus Prays

Christ Jesus who died—more than that,
who was raised to life—is at the right hand
of God and is also interceding for us.

Romans 8:34

Lord,

When I'm drowning in heavy emotions, it's difficult to pray. How do I articulate the depth of my pain? How do I ask for help when I'm too confused to know what I need? How can I focus my attention when exhaustion dulls my mind? I need You desperately, but I feel too weak to lift my hands to You in prayer.

I praise You for Jesus who "lives to intercede" and guarantee my forgiveness and salvation (Hebrews 7:25). He speaks my name in love. He cries out for mercy, help, and rescue from harm. No matter who might reject me or judge my life, Jesus stands up for me in heaven every moment. This truth is my comfort.

Amen.

Quiet Rest

When you lie down, you will not be afraid;
when you lie down, your sleep will be sweet.
Proverbs 3:24

Lord,

I dread the coming of night, knowing the hours of tension and fear I'll face before morning. My mind races with all the worst-case scenarios I can imagine. Others' needs and expectations fill me with stress. My problems loom large and seem impossible to overcome. I crave the relief of restorative sleep instead of this anxiety that wears me to the bone.

By Your Spirit, replace my fear with faith. Give me confidence in Your constant, watchful care. Show me how to place my worries in Your hands like a child who trusts a good and faithful Father. Interrupt these persistent nights of insomnia with sweet and quiet rest. Saturate my mind with Your promises to stay by my side so my anxieties give way to peace.

Amen.

"...you may have
peace in Me.
Here on earth you will have
many trials and sorrows.
But *take heart,* because
I have overcome the world."

John 16:33 NLT

6

Lasting Faith

We demolish arguments and every pretension that sets itself up against the knowledge of God, and we take captive every thought to make it obedient to Christ.

2 Corinthians 10:5

Lord,

My pain is not unique in this world. So many feel anxiety and crippling despair. Innocent ones are denied justice. Loved ones are lost, people's health fails, and hopes are disappointed. The world sets itself against You, laying the blame for suffering at Your feet. They deny Your Son, Jesus, who came to save and make all things new.

Guard my heart from giving in to doubt. Protect me from those who, like Job's wife, would tell me to curse You and give up on life (Job 2:9). Keep me holding on to Your "very great and precious promises" of a hope and a future forever with You (2 Peter 1:4). Anchor me in Your truth so I cannot be shaken.

Amen.

7

Safe and Secure

Keep me safe, O God,
for I have come to You for refuge.
Psalm 16:1 NLT

Lord,

It's easy to name the threats outside my door. This broken world holds hardship and loss at every hand. No person or place can fully insulate me from harm. Yet today, I realize the danger to myself is me.

When I tell myself that others would be better off without me, remind me I am chosen and purposed to "go and bear fruit" as I love in Your name (John 15:16-17). When I'm overwhelmed by despair, make me confident You are with me in this "darkest valley," leading me to the other side (Psalm 23:3-4). When I lose faith that my heart will ever heal, refresh my hope that "weeping may stay for the night, but rejoicing comes in the morning" (Psalm 30:5). Keep me safe in Your love that is greater than I can imagine.

Amen.

Follow His Lead

In their hearts humans plan their course,
but the LORD establishes their steps.
Proverbs 16:9

Lord,

It's tempting to think I know the path my life should take. When it veers off course, I grow angry or afraid. I hold up my ideals next to my reality, and I'm crushed by disappointment. It seems impossible to be happy and whole if my desires and dreams go unfulfilled.

Yet, Lord, who am I to doubt You as the Author of my life? How can I refuse to "participate in the sufferings of Christ" when those sufferings saved my soul (1 Peter 4:13)? How can I demand my own way when Your wisdom is good and perfect (Romans 12:2)? I am Your child. I want to follow wherever You lead. By Your Spirit, help me to surrender to Your plans and place my life in Your loving hands.

Amen.

9

Waiting for Morning

...weeping may stay for the night,
but rejoicing comes in the morning.
Psalm 30:5

Lord,

This night of depression feels like it will never end. Heavy emotions bury my joy and steal my hope for the future. The wounds of the past continue to hurt instead of heal. I've run out of tears to cry as I wait for rescue.

Yet in the middle of my darkest night, You promise the dawn of a new day. The weeping will end. Sorrows will be comforted. Fatigue will give way to energy and motivation. My relationships will flourish as we draw close to one another again. You will do a new work in my heart and mind so I walk in wisdom, truth, and peace.

Tonight, let me rest in Your promise of the joy to come. Shine Your light in my darkness. Open my heart to receive Your love.

Amen.

10

Guide My Way

You make known to me the path of life;
You will fill me with joy in Your presence,
with eternal pleasures at Your right hand.
Psalm 16:11

Lord,

I have no idea what's ahead. Will my relationships endure? Will I accomplish any of my hopes or dreams? Can I overcome the barriers that have held me back for so long? Will healing ever come? Is it possible to thrive in joy instead of struggling to survive?

Without You, I can't move forward. Speak through Your Word as a "lamp for my feet, a light on my path" (Psalm 119:105). Reveal which direction to turn toward help. Stir your passions in my heart so I know where to apply my time and energy. As I discover Your will for my life, fill me with gladness that comes from walking in step with Your Spirit. Be my source of joy and satisfaction.

Amen.

"For I know *the plans*
I have for you,"
says the LORD.
"They are plans *for good*
and not for disaster,
to give you a future
and *a hope*."
Jeremiah 29:11 NLT

My Strong Tower

I said, "Oh, that I had the wings of a dove!
I would fly away and be at rest."
Psalm 55:6

Lord,

When the pressures of life feel too intense, I want to cut and run. I'm eager to escape the never-ending list of obligations that fill my schedule. Anxieties rise, making me desperate to avoid those who threaten my security and wound my spirits. I want to flee from any source of pain and simply lie down and rest, with no one demanding a single thing.

I can't be all things to all people, Lord. My strength has limits. My defenses are weak. I'm easily overwhelmed and discouraged. Instead of running away, I need to run to You, my "strong tower against the foe" (Psalm 61:3). Be my refuge and protection from harm. Fill me with peace by Your Spirit. Let me find rest under Your wing.

Amen.

12

A Quiet Spirit

Fools vent their anger,
but the wise quietly hold it back.
Proverbs 29:11 NLT

Lord,

Under the weight of painful emotions, I find myself triggered by the most minor interruptions. Easily irritated, I lose my temper and lash out at those I love. I'm filled with regret at the hurt I've caused when anger takes control. It's clear I'm breaking trust and failing to love like You. I'm longing for peace in my heart and my home.

Forgive me, Lord, for sinning in my anger. Thank You for Your promise to save me and make me new. Bear Your Spirit's fruit of gentleness and self-control in my life (Galatians 5:22-23). Fill me with mercy and grace for others so I'm quick to listen and slow to become angry (James 1:19). Grow me in wisdom to stay calm and serve as a peacemaker wherever I go.

Amen.

Grow Me Up

...but we also glory in our sufferings, because we know that suffering produces perseverance; perseverance, character; and character, hope.

Romans 5:3-4

Lord,

In these dark days I keep asking, "Why?" Why do enjoyment and success seem out of reach? Why can others find secure, loving relationships but I suffer hurt and loss? Why must heavy emotions steal my joy and keep me tired, weak, and afraid? Why should I expect anything to change for the better? I need faith to believe that suffering is the path to hope in You.

Your Word holds the promise that You will not waste my pain. If I trust and depend on You, I can persevere. You will increase my strength, wisdom, and my compassion for others who struggle. I will know You more fully as You put Your love on display. Keep me holding on until hope comes to life in my heart.

Amen.

14

A Life Restored

"I will repay you for the years the locusts
have eaten...You will have plenty to eat,
until you are full, and you will praise
the name of the LORD your God,
who has worked wonders for you..."

Joel 2:25-26

Lord,

Depression has taken so much from my life. It has broken relationships and halted my progress. It canceled sweet times of fellowship and memories that could have been made. It made me question my worth and my future. Yet despite what's been lost, you can fill the days ahead with abundant life that overflows.

I'm grateful you will not let the past decide my future. Healing can be accomplished. Safe and loving relationships can build me up with joy. Doors can open to fresh opportunities. Forgiveness and grace can erase bitterness and tear down the walls around my heart. You are the God who works wonders for Your children, and Your love is my life.

Amen.

My God, My Champion

Let the heavens be glad, and the earth rejoice!
Tell all the nations, "The LORD reigns!"
1 Chronicles 16:31 NLT

Lord,

I feel I've lost every battle I fought to win. Hurtful people crash through the boundaries I set to protect my well-being. Past lies and unhealthy patterns creep back into my thoughts and behaviors. Attempts to move forward with goals or relationships take one step forward and two steps back. A cloud of defeat and failure casts a shadow over my life.

Restore my trust that You have the last word in all things—not my pain, not those against me, and not the losses of yesterday. Even now, You are keeping Your promise to make all things new. Help me to rejoice and "take heart" because You "have overcome the world" (John 16:33). I trust You as my Savior and King who fights for my victory.

Amen.

Jesus said, "*Come to Me,*
all of you who are weary
and carry heavy burdens,
and *I will give you rest.*"

Matthew 11:28 NLT

16

Sick and Sore

My life is consumed by anguish and my years by groaning; my strength fails because of my affliction, and my bones grow weak.

Psalm 31:10

Lord,

Heavy emotions take a toll on my body as well. Fatigue slows me down. Aches and pains steal my comfort. Disrupted sleep intensifies the tension, adding stress and strain to my days. I long to move with freedom and energy as I feel my strength draining away. My physical limits seem like a barrier to a full, meaningful life.

Thank You for drawing close to me in my weakness. Though it feels as if I can barely stand right now, I'm holding on to Your promise to renew my strength so I can "soar on wings like eagles" (Isaiah 40:31). Lord, soothe my sore muscles. Provide restorative sleep. Energize my mind and body. Make Your power perfect in my weakness as only You can (2 Corinthians 12:9).

Amen.

17

Always Loved

"He will take delight in you with gladness.
With His love, He will calm all your fears.
He will rejoice over you with joyful songs."
Zephaniah 3:17 NLT

Lord,

In my sadness, anger, and stress, I feel ugly and offensive to those around me. I have little to give. I worry I'm a burden. Will others grow tired of my tears? Is there more to me than my problems? I'm afraid I'll never feel whole and alive again.

Yet even as I'm afraid and insecure, You keep me as Your own. You declare that nothing can separate me from Your love (Romans 8:39). You are patient with my pace and forgiving of my failings. Help me to trust that it's Your delight to love me, help me, and comfort me as Your child. May I find joy in You as You rejoice over me today.

Amen.

A Friend of God

"I no longer call you servants, because a servant does not know his master's business. Instead, I have called you friends, for everything that I learned from My Father I have made known to you."

John 15:15

Lord,

I've never needed a friend like I do now. I need someone to trust. Someone who can carry the weight of my hurts and secrets. A friend who knows me through and through and loves me still. Someone who will never give up on me. I believed this friendship was impossible until I found You.

Thank You for calling me Yours. You give encouragement to carry on. In Your great love, You laid down Your life so I could live (1 John 3:16). You gave Your Spirit so I'm never alone. Your Word shares the truth of You and all You are to me. You have made all the difference.

Amen.

19

Be My Shield

Defend the weak and the fatherless;
uphold the cause of the poor and the
oppressed. Rescue the weak and the needy;
deliver them from the hand of the wicked.

Psalm 82:3-4

Lord,

Whether insults or abuse, betrayal or rejection, You know my sufferings at others' hands. The unjust have taken what I rightly deserved. The hateful have harmed me with cruel intent. The passive stood by while I struggled before their eyes. Those with much have taken no pity on my needs. I feel alone and defenseless as I wait for help to come.

You, Lord, hold my hopes in Your hands. Fulfill Your promise to protect and provide for me as Your child. Shield me from attack and uphold my name. Wrap me in love and friendship so I don't have to battle my problems alone. Let me know You as my strong Deliverer and the Healer of my heart.

Amen.

20

Lasting Love

For I am convinced that neither death
nor life, neither angels nor demons,
neither the present nor the future,
nor any powers, neither height nor depth,
nor anything else in all creation, will be
able to separate us from the love of God
that is in Christ Jesus our Lord.

Romans 8:38-39

Lord,

I confess that doubts whisper in my spirit, asking: Am I forgotten? Have I angered You by my weakness? Am I unworthy of Your help and care? Will I sink so low that You cannot reach me again? I need assurance that You will never let me go.

Renew my confidence in Your faithful love today. You watch over me every moment. Your ears are open to hear every cry and breath of prayer. When I'm rejected or accused, You call me chosen. Forgiven. Beloved. Nothing will diminish Your devotion to me as Your child. I believe.

Amen.

Trust in the LORD
with all your heart;
do not depend on your
own understanding.
Seek *His will* in all you do,
and He will show you
which *path to take*.

Proverbs 3:5-6 NLT

Brave Love

There is no fear in love. But perfect love drives out fear, because fear has to do with punishment.

1 John 4:18

Lord,

I never knew what love looked like until I found You. Others made me work for their attention. If I failed, I was rejected. My needs were disregarded or treated as a burden. I had no one to cheer me on or help me to imagine all the joys my life might hold. I built walls around my heart to protect me from the hurts that were sure to come.

Thank You for Your perfect love that never ends. Turn my fear to faith in Your kindness and mercy. Help me to better understand the powerful work of Jesus on the cross that rescued me from guilt and shame. Break down every barrier that holds me back from running to Your open arms. Fill me with Your peace.

Amen.

22

A Place to Belong

Jesus replied, "All who love Me will do what I say.
My Father will love them, and We will come
and make Our home with each of them."

John 14:23 NLT

Lord,

Sometimes I wonder where I belong. I feel like I'm on the outside looking in, disconnected from everyone around me. I long to feel wanted, secure, and at rest. I'm grateful that as Your child I can be always at home with You.

When I remain in You, all is well. Help me to believe Your promises and submit to Your Word. Teach me what it means to abide in You and know You as my Father and Friend. When feelings of fear or loneliness rise up in my heart, reassure me that I'm kept safe under Your wing. You are always faithful in Your love—keep me faithful to You as I surrender to You in everything.

Amen.

Strength to Endure

We are hard pressed on every side, but not crushed; perplexed, but not in despair; persecuted, but not abandoned; struck down, but not destroyed.

2 Corinthians 4:8-9

Lord,

I'm grateful for the Scripture verses that put words to the stress, confusion, and sorrow I face. You see the pressure I feel to achieve a strength I don't possess. You show compassion when I struggle to believe my story can have a happy ending. When it seems everyone is against me, You know my loneliness and fear. My heart is an open book to You, and You love me through and through.

Thank You for Your promise to sustain me in this dark season. You will not allow pain or evil to have the last word in my life. I may feel broken, but You will carry me, help me, and stay by my side. You are my hope who never fails.

Amen.

24

Show the Way

If any of you lacks wisdom, you should ask God, who gives generously to all without finding fault, and it will be given to you.

James 1:5

Lord,

My emotions are constantly changing—it's as if they take on a life of their own. I'm tempted to believe that what feels true is true. When I'm feeling low, I slip into despair that denies Your faithful love. When I feel a rush of confidence, I think I'm strong enough to make it without Your help. I need You to plant my feet on the solid ground of Your truth and wisdom each day.

Guide my steps as I pursue healing and life-giving relationships that build me up. Reveal any habits or mindsets that are keeping me from trusting and obeying Your Word. Shape my goals and priorities. Supply the help I need. Lead me in Your way of love.

Amen.

Patiently Waiting

Be joyful in hope, patient in
affliction, faithful in prayer.

Romans 12:12

Lord,

I thought by now I'd be free. Free from depression. Free from hurtful, complicated relationships. Free to pursue my hopes and dreams without anything holding me back. I thought I'd be well and strong and healed from my past. I'm struggling to hold on to hope and trust that joy is on the way.

Bear Your Spirit's fruit of patience in me so I can endure my difficulties without giving up. Refresh my hope that You are using each struggle to teach me, grow me, and reveal Your faithful love. Draw me to You every day in prayer, knowing You listen and respond to the cries of my heart. Fill me with joy that comes from knowing You are utterly for me. You will sustain me and bless me as Your beautiful plan unfolds for my life.

Amen.

Give all your worries
and cares to *God*,
for *He cares about you.*

1 Peter 5:7 NLT

Saved by Grace

But when the kindness and love of God our Savior appeared, He saved us, not because of righteous things we had done, but because of His mercy.

Titus 3:4-5

Lord,

Because of You, I have a soft place to land. I don't have to pretend I'm perfect. I'm released from the pressure to earn Your attention. My sins—no matter how shameful or foolish—cannot diminish Your mercy toward me. Because of Jesus, the floodgates of Your love wash over my life.

I never want to doubt Your grace that has saved me, redeemed me, and made me new. May I follow and obey because I trust You with all my heart. Protect me from past fears of rejection and punishment that deny Your kindness and silence my prayers. Give me humility to listen, learn, and depend on You. Overwhelm me with Your love that never fails.

Amen.

27

God Is Good

I remain confident of this:
I will see the goodness of the
LORD in the land of the living.
Psalm 27:13

Lord,

Just when I think my life has reached its capacity for pain, I suffer yet another blow. My support system is crumbling. Setbacks keep blessings out of reach. My situation goes from bad to worse, and I can't imagine how I'll take hold of peace or joy again.

Yet You, my God, promise Your love cannot be overcome. In that love, You say I can find security. Mercy and compassion. Victory. Healing and help. You promise Your divine power that gives all I need to keep trusting and carry on (2 Peter 1:3).

"I do believe; help me overcome my unbelief!" (Mark 9:24). Fill me with confidence that I will see Your goodness both in this life and the life to come. Overwhelm me with Your love.

Amen.

God's Open Arms

Because of Christ and our faith in Him, we can now come boldly and confidently into God's presence.

Ephesians 3:12 NLT

Lord,

Depression leaves me feeling like a broken mess. I wish I could power through my fatigue and heavy emotions. I'm ashamed each time I give in to fear. Despite my progress, I fall back into unhealthy mindsets and habits of the past. It's hard to love myself and sometimes harder to trust You love me as I am.

By Your Spirit, build my confidence in Your "perfect love" that "drives out fear, because fear has to do with punishment" (1 John 4:18). You are for me. You'll never reject me or let me go. Because of Jesus, I'm forgiven and saved as Your child for all time. Your love is constant and true. May I believe You so fully that I run to Your open arms each day.

Amen.

29

Stronger with You

The Lord will guide you always;
He will satisfy your needs in
a sun-scorched land and
will strengthen your frame.
Isaiah 58:11

Lord,

I'm empty. I've worked and worried until my strength is gone. I ignored my need for rest, for help, and for compassion. I tried to be all things to all people until I had nothing left to give. Now, I feel defeated and too weak to carry on. I need You like never before.

Help me to know You as my tender, loving Father. Work in my heart so I believe that in You, I'm cherished and accepted, seen and known. Show me a better way forward, where I no longer carry burdens that are not mine to bear. Erase the lie that says my needs don't matter. Build me back up so I can live with purpose and joy. In You, I am whole.

Amen.

Yours Forever

For He has rescued us from the
dominion of darkness and brought us
into the kingdom of the Son He loves.
Colossians 1:13

Lord,

You knew I needed a hero. The enemy had me trapped in fear. His lies convinced me I was weak, worthless, and doomed to be alone. I felt too ashamed to cry out to You for mercy and forgiveness. I had no hope. No future. No strength to overcome. Yet You found me in the darkness and called me into Your wonderful light (1 Peter 2:9).

May I never doubt so great a salvation. When I'm tempted to fall back into shame or self-hatred, overwhelm me with Your love. Help me to stand firm when the enemy tempts me with sin to bring me back into bondage. Give me unshakeable faith in Your Word that says I am Yours and You are mine.

Amen.

Even when I walk
through the darkest valley,
I will not be afraid,
for You are *close beside me.*
Your rod and Your staff
protect and comfort me.

Psalm 23:4 NLT

Keep Me Close

"I am the vine; you are the branches.
If you remain in Me and I in you, you will bear
much fruit; apart from Me you can do nothing."
John 15:5

Lord,

You know the pressure I put on myself. I want to be someone others can count on. I'm crushed each time I lose control of my emotions, fail to meet my goals, or fall short of the ideals I've created in my mind. I've believed the lie that strength and willpower can accomplish what only You can in my life.

I need Your forgiveness for my self-sufficient pride. Teach me to trust You to complete the work You've begun to make me new. Keep me faithful in prayer so I ask for Your help and listen to Your voice. Grow and change me through Your Word. Bear Your fruit of love in my life as I remain in You.

Amen.

32

Joy Is on the Way

And the God of all grace, who called you
to His eternal glory in Christ, after you have
suffered a little while, will Himself restore you
and make you strong, firm and steadfast.

1 Peter 5:10

Lord,

Pain and sorrow go on and on with no relief. When I try to climb out of the pit, I sink even deeper than before. I grow afraid that I'll never mend. My heart yearns for peace and to experience the joys of life once more.

Help me to trust You are holding me and carrying me to freedom even now. Give me a fresh assurance that "weeping may stay for the night, but rejoicing comes in the morning" (Psalm 30:5). Sustain a tenacious faith that believes in Jesus' power to save. Restore my hope. Fill me with "inexpressible and glorious joy" by Your Spirit (1 Peter 1:8). Your love is life.

Amen.

33

Beloved Child

See what great love the Father has
lavished on us, that we should be called
children of God! And that is what we are!

1 John 3:1

Lord,

In my griefs I can forget my own name. I look in the mirror and all I can see is sad. Broken. Depressed. Hopeless. Afraid. Lonely. My emotions cloud the truth of who I am in You.

Help me to remember Your lavish love. Open my eyes to see Your faithful care in the middle of my suffering. Set me free from guilt and shame that deny Your mercy, forgiveness, and the salvation of my soul. Let me take hold of my identity as Your chosen and precious child. Protect me from those who would shake my confidence in Your powerful presence in my life. I am Yours and You are mine, and this makes all the difference. I love You.

Amen.

34

The Good Shepherd

"I will be like a shepherd looking for
his scattered flock. I will find My sheep
and rescue them from all the places where
they were scattered on that dark and cloudy day."

Ezekiel 34:12 NLT

Lord,

My heart is longing for a sense of home where I'm loved and know I belong. Others know my name, but they don't know my greatest hurts or the hopes of my heart. It's hard to keep the faith without the encouragement and care of sincere believers. I feel isolated and defenseless in this storm. I can't make it alone.

Let me know You as my Shepherd who rescues me from harm. Carry me to safety and renew my trust in You. Show me Your love among the "family of believers" You've knit together for all time (1 Peter 2:17). Give peace through the assurance that You watch and keep me as Your own. You are my safe place.

Amen.

35

Where Help Comes From

"LORD, You establish peace for us; all that we have accomplished You have done for us."

Isaiah 26:12

Lord,

Everywhere I look, someone claims to know the path to peace. Some say it's through achievement and wealth. Others look to health or a fit, attractive image. Romance, travel, a simple and beautiful home, knowledge—all of these are offered as a cure for the chaos I feel inside. Yet nothing I have or do can achieve the peace I'm desperate to find.

Only You can quiet my fears. It's only through Jesus that I can be healed. Protected. Forgiven. Comforted. Made new. Your peace is a gift of love, not a payment for hard work in my own strength. The peace I find in You doesn't melt away in the heat of trouble. Thank You, Father, for drawing me close and soothing my soul. This is grace.

Amen.

"Be strong
and courageous!
Do not be afraid
or discouraged.
For the LORD your God
is with you
wherever you go."

Joshua 1:9 NLT

Willing to Change

Wounds from a friend can be trusted, but an enemy multiplies kisses...Perfume and incense bring joy to the heart, and the pleasantness of a friend springs from their heartfelt advice.

Proverbs 27:6, 9

Lord,

I don't always get it right. My emotions cloud my understanding of what's true and real. False assumptions create conflict and unnecessary pain. My limited perspective keeps me from seeing the help and resources You've given for my good. I need a caring, honest friend who will tell me what I need to hear.

I pray You will send others to speak the truth in love instead of offering quick fixes or false sympathy. Give me a humble spirit that is willing to be corrected and challenged to change. Teach me Your Word so Your wisdom and light can shine into my life. Thank You that I don't have to walk this road alone.

Amen.

37

Ready to Repent

Godly sorrow brings repentance that
leads to salvation and leaves no regret,
but worldly sorrow brings death.

2 Corinthians 7:10

Lord,

My words have wounded the ones I love. I've broken promises and damaged trust. I let my problems consume my attention, so I ignored the hurts of others around me. I turned down help when it was offered and chose to sit in my misery. I've sinned, and this grieves my heart.

Yet Lord, this sorrow can easily spiral into shame that feeds my depression and drives me far from You. Fill me instead with godly grief that moves me to confess. To repent. To rely on Your mercy and receive Your forgiveness. To be set free. As I turn from my sins, let me turn to You and find the love and hope I've been searching for all along. You are my joy, forever.

Amen.

38

Shine Your Light

In Him was life, and that life was the light
of all mankind. The light shines in the darkness,
and the darkness has not overcome it.
John 1:4-5

Lord,

If anyone understands this darkness, it's You. You know the wrongs I suffered. You read my thoughts and feel the emotions I carry inside. You've heard every lie the enemy has whispered in my ears to feed my despair. You see my crumbling hope and my fear that I'll fall apart. The darkness cannot hide any part of me from Your loving eyes.

You, Lord, are my light and salvation. Evil and pain are no match for Your power. You will not let anything snatch me from Your hand because You've claimed me as Your own. When sin was dragging me toward death, You saved me through Jesus. May I live as a "child of light" in Your love (Ephesians 5:8).

Amen.

39

Fear or Faith?

Jesus responded, "Why are you afraid? You have so little faith!" Then He got up and rebuked the wind and waves, and suddenly there was a great calm.

Matthew 8:26 NLT

Lord,

Depression has removed all sense of safety from my life. I'm afraid I'll come to harm. When healing is slow to come, I fear I'll be trapped in misery forever. I wonder if others will grow tired of my struggle and abandon me to suffer alone. A cloud of disaster hangs over my future and I'm desperate for help.

By Your Spirit, give me what I need to trust Your power and love. Quiet my panic. Give me signs You are working faithfully to mend what's broken inside. Fill me with courage as I believe You are by my side through whatever I face. "Keep me safe, my God, for in You I take refuge" (Psalm 16:1).

Amen.

You Satisfy

"Why spend money on what is not bread,
and your labor on what does not satisfy?
Listen, listen to Me, and eat what is good,
and you will delight in the richest of fare."
Isaiah 55:2

Lord,

The world is quick to offer food, money, and pleasure to soothe my pain. Screens and busyness distract me from the healing work that's needed in my heart and mind. I confess I crave a quick fix instead of the slow, head-to-toe transformation You aim to accomplish by Your Spirit. It's time for me to listen, learn, and put You first in my life.

Turn my apathy to hunger for Your Word. When I'm anxious or downhearted, draw me close and keep me on my knees in prayer. Surround me with those who trust You, praise You, and follow where You lead. Rescue me from a futile life that's empty of You.

Amen.

I waited patiently
for the LORD to help me,
and He turned to me
and heard my cry.
He lifted me out
of the pit of despair,
out of the mud
and the mire.
He set my feet
on solid ground
and steadied me
as I walked along.

Psalm 40:1-2 NLT

Caring Comfort

Praise be to...the God of all comfort,
who comforts us in all our troubles, so that
we can comfort those in any trouble with
the comfort we ourselves receive from God.

2 Corinthians 1:3-4

Lord,

Fear, sadness, and stress will lead me down one of two roads: I will become bitter and hardhearted, or I'll be humble and compassionate to those who suffer. I pray You will use the test of my troubles to refine me like silver so I reflect Your wonderful love (Psalm 66:10).

Thank You for Your comfort and tender heart toward my pain. You keep me close, hear my prayers, and count each tear I cry. Use me to comfort those who feel depressed or overwhelmed by the world's darkness. Help me to be vulnerable with my hurts so others can be open with their own. Show me how to listen and love like Jesus.

Amen.

42

Caring for Others

Love is patient, love is kind. It does not envy, it does not boast, it is not proud.

1 Corinthians 13:4

Lord,

At times it seems that others' burdens are light compared to the pain I have to bear. Rather than celebrating the happiness of people around me, I crave their blessings for myself. It's tempting to slip into self-pity instead of loving and caring about those around me.

As Your child, I want to love as You've loved me. I'm eager to bear Your Spirit's fruit of kindness and goodness to everyone You place in my life. I pray You will guard my heart from coveting and counting others' blessings instead of my own. Keep me from a martyr mentality that demands special treatment. Instead, use my suffering to grow a spirit of compassion in my heart so I listen, serve, and offer comfort in Your name.

Amen.

Never the Same

This means that anyone who belongs
to Christ has become a new person.
The old life is gone; a new life has begun!
2 Corinthians 5:17 NLT

Lord,

In my struggle for mental health, I feel I've lost ground in my life. My stamina and confidence have weakened. My trust in others has grown insecure. Instead of dreaming about the future's possibilities, I'm just trying to make it through the day. Yet as my Savior and loving God, You promise that even now You are making me new.

Restore my faith that in Jesus, I am no longer guilty. The power of sin and evil has been broken. I am Yours, and nothing can separate me from You. The past cannot define my identity or my future. The Spirit is filling me with love, joy, and peace that doesn't depend on my circumstances. Because of You I'll never be the same.

Amen.

44

An Abundant Life

"The thief comes only to steal and kill
and destroy; I have come that they
may have life, and have it to the full."
John 10:10

Lord,

Depression is hard. Yet it's so much worse when the enemy uses it to steal my peace. My trust in You. Confidence in my identity as Your child. Strength to pursue healing, prayer, and time in Your Word. The enemy tempts me to feel self-pity and make excuses for sin. He's determined to kill my faith and destroy my life.

I'm grateful that You're on my side no matter the dangers I face. You make me brave in faith with "power, love and self-discipline" by Your Spirit (2 Timothy 1:7). You erase the enemy's lies with truth that never fails. When I'm accused and ashamed, You declare I am forgiven and righteous in Your sight. You are my light and life.

Amen.

A Word of Kindness

Anxiety weighs down the heart,
but a kind word cheers it up.
Proverbs 12:25

Lord,

You know how my struggles leave me overwhelmed and alone. I lose my joy. My outlook grows negative and hopeless. I feel I cast a shadow over others' happiness, so I pull away to carry my burdens alone. Today my heart is heavy as I crave a word of kindness. A smile. A taste of friendship to remind my spirit that I'm seen and loved.

I pray You'll send someone to cross my path who has Your heart of care. May their words shine Your light through the clouds of depression. Use them to ease my loneliness and cheer up my day. Refresh my hope that today's struggles will move behind me as a beautiful future is yet to come. You're here, You're faithful, and Your love surrounds my life.

Amen.

"Don't be afraid,
for I am with you.
Don't be discouraged,
for I am your God.
I will *strengthen* you
and *help* you.
I will hold you up with
My victorious right hand."

Isaiah 41:10 NLT

Hope for Tomorrow

There is surely a future hope for you,
and your hope will not be cut off.
Proverbs 23:18

Lord,

If my future rested on my own shoulders, I'd have no hope at all. My wisdom is too limited to show which way to go. Despite my best intentions, I fall into temptation and doubt. I cannot rewrite the past or heal what's broken. I can't earn my way to heaven no matter how I strain after perfection. You—and only You—are where hope is found.

Thank You for constant assurance that I'm Yours and You'll never let me go. I praise You for Jesus "who loved me and gave Himself for me" so I could be with You always (Galatians 2:20). Nothing will separate me from Your love. Today's sadness and stress will give way to an eternity of perfect joy and peace. This hope changes everything.

Amen.

47

A Humble Heart

Do not be wise in your own eyes; fear the LORD and shun evil. This will bring health to your body and nourishment to your bones.

Proverbs 3:7-8

Lord,

You know how others have treated me badly and hurt my heart. You've heard my cries when depression crushed all joy and strength, leaving me desperate for relief. It's tempting to focus on my circumstances—or others' failings toward me—instead of my faith and obedience to You.

I confess that in my pride I often claim to know the best solutions to my problems. My hard heart needs Your grace to forgive just as You've forgiven me. I neglect Your powerful Word that is "God-breathed and is useful for teaching, rebuking, correcting and training in righteousness" (2 Timothy 3:16-17).

Restore a humble heart in me that depends on Your wisdom and submits to all You say. Life and healing are found in You.

Amen.

Satisfy My Soul

Yet true godliness with contentment is itself great wealth. After all, we brought nothing with us when we came into the world, and we can't take anything with us when we leave it.
1 Timothy 6:6-7 NLT

Lord,

I yearn for what I've lost. Nothing can answer the "why" of what's happened in my life. Sadness lingers without relief. No amount of distraction can ease the heavy ache in my chest or keep the tears away for long. I don't know how to make peace with the pain. By Your Spirit, let me discover the "secret of living in every situation" with a contented heart (Philippians 4:12).

Show me how to hold deep sorrow and great hope at the same time. Reassure me of Your love and build my faith to believe You will make all things new. As I come to You in my weakness, fill me with strength to endure. Be the One who satisfies my soul.

Amen.

49

You Are Enough

I know what it is to be in need, and I know what it is to have plenty. I have learned the secret of being content in any and every situation, whether well fed or hungry, whether living in plenty or in want.

Philippians 4:12

Lord,

I'm weary of this persistent sorrow. My energy fades before I make it through the day. I long for the comfort of loving, supportive relationships. I crave a sense of worth and purpose. But for now, I feel needy. Empty. Joyless. I struggle to trust and wait for the good You have in store.

I pray for grace to be content no matter my circumstances. May I find such satisfaction in You that nothing else compares. When I wrestle with wants and desires, give me a patient and grateful spirit that trusts You for all I need. Be my hope and my first love.

Amen.

On My Side

God is just: He will pay back trouble to those who trouble you and give relief to you who are troubled, and to us as well.

2 Thessalonians 1:6-7

Lord,

I struggle to come to terms with all I've suffered. Why does my abuser seem to thrive while my wounds have yet to heal? Why is my voice silenced and my boundaries ignored? Why am I held to a high standard while others can treat me as they please? I need relief, and I need to trust You will stand for me until the end.

Help me to believe You are on my side because I'm loved, I'm redeemed, and I'm Yours. Build my faith in Your power to work justice for the past and protect me from future harm. Guard my heart from bitterness so I can forgive as You've forgiven me. You are my champion and my peace.

Amen.

The Lord is close
to the brokenhearted;
He rescues those
whose spirits are crushed.

Psalm 34:18 NLT

Better Together

Look to the LORD and His strength;
seek His face always.
1 Chronicles 16:11

Lord,

I'm fragile. The lightest burden feels like a crushing weight, keeping me from standing up and stepping forward in my life. Daily decisions leave me confused and unsure of what to do. I feel weak and powerless in the face of what's required of me each day.

The moment I let go of Your hand, I fall. Teach me to abide in You and seek Your face. Keep me constant in prayer so Your strength keeps me going. Turn my attention to Your Word so its truth can renew my mind and refresh my hope. Move me to gather with Your people who build me up and inspire praise to You. May I set aside any foolish attempts to stand on my own so I depend on You and receive all I need.

Amen.

52

Trust and Obey

The precepts of the LORD are right,
giving joy to the heart. The commands of
the LORD are radiant, giving light to the eyes.

Psalm 19:8

Lord,

Each time I choose my own way, it disappoints. The goals I pursue leave me disillusioned. Others' attention or approval fails to satisfy my need for deep love and connection.

Medical support falls short in fully healing my body or mind. The world's priorities and values leave me stuck in guilt and regret. I need rock-solid wisdom and truth that will never let me down.

Forgive me for resisting Your authority. Teach me Your Word. Humble my heart so I follow Your lead and say "yes" to whatever You say. By Your Spirit, help me understand how to pursue healing and relate with the people in my life. Bless me with the joy of a clean conscience, insight, and confidence in You.

Amen.

Passing the Test

No discipline seems pleasant at the time, but painful. Later on, however, it produces a harvest of righteousness and peace for those who have been trained by it.

Hebrews 12:11

Lord,

The pain I suffer today is testing my faith. Will I believe You are good and trust You're in control? Can I hold on to hope? Will I listen and obey, even when I don't understand? Is Your love better to me than anything in this world? Help me to endure as You do Your work in my life.

I pray You will teach me to trust You like never before. Soften my heart so I'm compassionate to others who suffer. Grow my patience as I wait for Your rescue. Fill me with peace that doesn't depend on my circumstances. Give me eyes to see Your light in the darkness. Your love will not let me go.

Amen.

54

Keep Believing

See to it that no one takes you captive through hollow and deceptive philosophy, which depends on human tradition and the elemental spiritual forces of this world rather than on Christ.

Colossians 2:8

Lord,

When I'm feeling low, it's easy to let down my guard. The enemy finds cracks in my armor and tempts me to doubt Your Word. I slip into worldly thinking that says to "find my truth." To stand on my own two feet. To impress for success. To put myself first. To deny my Lord Jesus. Yet the way of the world can never save or satisfy like Your way of love.

Keep me safe from those who would undermine my faith. Give me courage to follow You, even if I walk that path alone. Guide me in Your wisdom as I search for help and healing. Keep me faithful to the end. I love You.

Amen.

55

The One to Trust

Why, my soul, are you downcast?
Why so disturbed within me?
Put your hope in God, for I will yet
praise Him, my Savior and my God.
Psalm 43:5

Lord,

Life brings painful losses. Friends and loved ones betray my trust. Dreams give way to disappointment. The struggles can feel overwhelming and I lose my strength to cope. Dark and negative thoughts consume my mind, and I fear more suffering might come my way.

I need You to replace my fear with faith in You, my Savior. Help me to remember Your faithfulness in the past. You have never left my side. You listen to every cry of my heart. No difficulty is able to separate me from Your love (Romans 8:35-36). Fill me with hope as I wait for Your comfort and help. You are my strength and my peace, and You are worthy of all my praise.

Amen.

The Lord directs
the steps of the godly.
He delights in
every detail of their lives.
Though they stumble,
they will never fall,
for *the Lord holds them*
by the hand.

Psalm 37:23-24 NLT

Dry My Tears

"I will turn their mourning into gladness;
I will give them comfort and joy instead of sorrow."
Jeremiah 31:13

Lord,

I'm holding on to Your promises as my lifeline today. You love me too much to leave me in despair. Though others wounded my heart and pushed me away, You draw me close to comfort and mend what's broken. When I lost what I held most dear, You gave me priceless treasures in Jesus that truly satisfy. I know as I keep trusting and loving You, You will fill me "with an inexpressible and glorious joy" (1 Peter 1:8).

Sustain my faith, Lord, that mourning will give way to gladness in my life. You will dry my tears. You'll open my eyes to see how good and faithful You've been from the start. My life's story will tell of Your love and how with You, all things are possible.

Amen.

57

Stronger with You

So I say, walk by the Spirit, and you
will not gratify the desires of the flesh.
Galatians 5:16

Lord,

As my struggle goes on and on, I want to numb the pain. I'm tempted to distract my thoughts with mindless entertainment. Food and sleep become easy comforts when I'm tired, sick, and sore. I choose the ease of isolation instead of investing in relationships that build me up. My flesh craves relief that only You can provide.

I need a pure heart so I no longer self-medicate with substitutes for Your truth and love. Teach me to walk by the Spirit instead of giving in to destructive desires. Give me strength to pray and meditate on Your Word each day. Guide me to rest, move, and nourish my body in healthy and beneficial ways. Be my source of strength so I rely on You alone.

Amen.

Forgiven and Free

Therefore, there is now no condemnation
for those who are in Christ Jesus.
Romans 8:1

Lord,

Depression has thrown me into a pit of shame. Inner accusations label me as selfish and ungrateful. Weak and immature. Small in faith. Lazy and useless. A burden to my loved ones. Unworthy of Your love. The guilt just deepens my despair as it drives me away from You.

Renew my trust in Your unconditional love. Let me know You as my merciful Father. Relieve my doubts and fill me with fresh hope, "For the LORD comforts His people and will have compassion on His afflicted ones" (Isaiah 49:13). Assure my heart that because of Christ, You see me as beloved, blameless, and new.

Silence the accusations and fill my mind with truth. I am forgiven and free. You never let me go. Nothing will separate me from Your love.

Amen.

59

My Perfect Teacher

May my cry come before You, LORD;
give me understanding according to Your word.
Psalm 119:169

Lord,

Your compassion comforts my soul. You hear my cries of grief, regret, and fear when emotions overwhelm my heart and mind. In Your wisdom, You know the true source of my pain and the path I need to walk toward healing.

In the confusing swirl of feelings, I can't trust my own perceptions of what's happened in my life. I wonder, *Have I grown bitter? Am I safeguarding myself from hurtful people? Do I resist the help You've provided?* Enable me to see rightly so my responses and plans, words and desires are shaped by what's true. Use Your Word to teach me wise understanding to cope in my struggles each day. I want to think Your thoughts and follow Jesus' example of perfect love and obedience to You.

Amen.

Seen and Known

Search me, O God, and know my heart;
test me and know my anxious thoughts.
Psalm 139:23 NLT

Lord,

My outward reactions hint of inner wounds yet to heal. I push painful emotions, hard questions, and traumatic memories down as far as I can, but they rise once more to torment my soul. I'm tempted to use physical pleasures and distractions to numb my feelings and escape my thoughts. But You, Lord, fully comprehend who I am and what's broken inside.

It's time to stop hiding from the truth. Examine my heart and mind with Your loving eyes. Give me courage to face each fear and doubt, sin and sorrow You reveal. I trust that in my blindness, You "will turn the darkness into light before [me] and make the rough places smooth" (Isaiah 42:16). By Your power, make me new and joyful and free.

Amen.

The LORD hears
His people when they
call to Him for help.
He rescues them
from all their troubles.

Psalm 34:17 NLT

A New Heart

"For I will forgive their wickedness
and will remember their sins no more."
Hebrews 8:12

Lord,

Memories of the past feel fresh and raw. So many times, I was stubborn and went my own way. I looked for love apart from You. My desires and attitudes were shaped by the world instead of Your Word and Spirit. I was driven by fear instead of faith in Your promises. My sins made me hide in shame instead of running to You for mercy and forgiveness. Without Your love, I would be lost.

Thank You for washing me clean and making me new. "Restore to me the joy of Your salvation" when I'm tempted by doubt and shame (Psalm 51:12). Teach me what it means to be Yours—chosen, beloved, and righteous in Jesus—so I trust You more and more. Give me a faith that cannot be shaken.

Amen.

62

A Call for Help

But as for me, I am poor and needy; may the
LORD think of me. You are my help and my
deliverer; You are my God, do not delay.

Psalm 40:17

Lord,

I feel I've reached my breaking point. I'm lost in the darkness of hurt, fear, and despair. Weak and exhausted, I don't have the strength to fight for life and joy any longer. I cannot carry on without Your help. You are my only hope.

Put Your arms around me, Lord, and set me back on my feet. Restore my hope in the future You've already planned for my life. Let me know You as my Rescuer, my Champion, and "the One who lifts my head high" (Psalm 3:3). Wash away my doubts and discouragement so I trust You with all my heart. You are mighty and faithful. Your love has never let me go.

Amen.

The Goodness of God

"I do not give to you as the world gives. Do not let your hearts be troubled and do not be afraid."
John 14:27

Lord,

In this world, you're loved if you're successful and live up to people's expectations. You're told you'll find peace through acceptance, prosperity, and freedom to do whatever you want. Yet no matter how I try, I can never earn perfect love and devotion from others. It's impossible to craft a life that's shielded from pain or struggle. It's clear that my soul will never be satisfied apart from You.

I'm grateful Your blessings are gifts of grace instead of payments for perfect behavior. Your Spirit can fill me with joy no matter my circumstances. You keep Your promise to love me fully and stay with me every moment. I can trust Your goodness completely so I never have to be afraid. Thank You for Your peace.

Amen.

Be a Blessing

The generous will prosper;
those who refresh others will
themselves be refreshed.
Proverbs 11:25 NLT

Lord,

In this season of weakness, I feel I have so little to give. My energy is low. Healing requires time and focus. As I carry my heavy burdens, I wonder how I can help others to bear their own. Yet Lord, I still want to somehow make a difference and share Your love.

Open my eyes to recognize the "good works" You "prepared in advance" for me to do (Ephesians 2:10). Reveal how I am to share the gifts and resources You have provided in my life. Give me sensitivity to the hurts and worries of others so I can come alongside with caring friendship. Despite my limitations, show me how I am needed, useful, and called to serve like Jesus. May I experience soul-lifting blessings as I bless others in Your name.

Amen.

Make Me New

Do not conform to the pattern of this world,
but be transformed by the renewing of your mind.
Romans 12:2

Lord,

The world says I have a right to be bitter, and that I'll be happy if I get what I want. The world says it's foolish to trust in Jesus. It puts the burden to be strong and healed on my own shoulders. Yet if I conform to the world, I'll never know Your love and power. Only You can do the work of transformation I so desperately need today.

Renew my mind so I see my life through Your eyes. Move me from despair to hope, shame to forgiveness, and fear to courage. Give me confidence that Your will is "good, pleasing, and perfect" for me in every way (Romans 12:2). Help me to understand Your truth so I can build my life on its firm foundation.

Amen.

You, O Lord,
are a shield around me;
You *are my glory,*
the One who *holds*
my head high.

Psalm 3:3 NLT

Build Me Up

Therefore encourage one another and build each other up, just as in fact you are doing.
1 Thessalonians 5:11

Lord,

The path of life is too difficult to walk alone. I grow tired and discouraged. Pressures build until I'm too stressed and anxious to function. The world and the enemy's lies leave me confused and insecure. I need other believers to keep reminding me of Your love and truth so I can heal, grow, and stay faithful to You.

Build me up through the kindness of others today. Send someone as Your messenger with a word of hope. Use a godly voice to break through my negative, destructive thoughts and set me back on the firm ground of Your Word. Let me experience Your loving care through the ministry of Your people. And even as I receive help and comfort, use me to encourage others around me.

Amen.

67

God's Healing Word

He has sent me to bind up the brokenhearted…

Isaiah 61:1

Lord,

At times I feel too sick and sad to form the words to pray. Thank You for Your Word that names my needs, my longings, and the cries of my heart. Today I cling to Jesus who fulfilled the Scriptures in Isaiah 61:

"…the Lord has anointed me
  to proclaim good news to the poor.
He has sent me to bind up the brokenhearted,
  to proclaim freedom for the captives
  and release from darkness for the prisoners…
to comfort all who mourn,
  and provide for those who grieve in Zion—
to bestow on them a crown of beauty
  instead of ashes,
the oil of joy instead of mourning,
and a garment of praise
  instead of a spirit of despair" (vv. 1-3).

The good news of Jesus is my hope and my life.

Amen.

Never Give Up

"In this world you will have trouble.
But take heart! I have overcome the world."
John 16:33

Lord,

I wonder how far I can bend before I break. People can be cruel. Bad news strikes without warning. Stress and pressure wear me down. Painful emotions become so overwhelming, it's hard to function. I feel foolish for thinking I'd be spared the troubles of this life. I know now that I cannot endure on my own.

Thank You for shining Your light into the darkness all around me. You offer comfort and hope. Your power can overcome every danger, enemy, and struggle I face. When I don't know where to run for safety, You are "my refuge, a strong tower against the foe" (Psalm 61:3). You get the last word over evil. Nothing can separate me from Your love or snatch me from Your hand. You're my constant hope.

Amen.

69

Jesus Understands

He was despised and rejected by mankind,
a Man of suffering, and familiar with pain.
Isaiah 53:3

Lord,

You know how it feels to be slandered and abused. Friends promised love and loyalty, only to abandon You in Your darkest hour. Others only wanted to use You for their own gain. You suffered brutality. Injustice. Fatigue and hunger. Temptation. Because of the wounds You endured, You understand my hurt in every detail.

I pray I will know Your victory just as You know my pain. Show me the power of Jesus' resurrection (Philippians 3:10). Defeat the power of sin and darkness in my life. Complete the "good work" You began to make me new (Philippians 1:6). Give me strength to endure my struggles and use them to help me know Jesus more and more. Thank You for Your gift of love and life that nothing can take away.

Amen.

Renew My Mind

...whatever is true, whatever is noble, whatever is right, whatever is pure, whatever is lovely, whatever is admirable—if anything is excellent or praiseworthy—think about such things.

Philippians 4:8

Lord,

My thoughts are an open book to You. You know how I dwell on past hurts and disappointments. You're aware that I compare myself to others and tear myself down. I can't hide my inner complaints, self-pity, or the doubt that joy will ever come my way. My thoughts so often deny Your beautiful promises to love, rescue, and care for me as Your child.

Renew my mind by Your Spirit so I meditate on what is right and good. Saturate my thoughts with Your Word. Keep me focused on all the ways You give help and comfort when I'm feeling low. Teach me to name what is "excellent or praiseworthy" in myself as Your cherished creation. May I be ever captivated with You.

Amen.

Those who know
Your name
trust in You,
for You, O LORD,
do not abandon
those who
search for You.
Psalm 9:10 NLT

Refresh My Soul

"I will refresh the weary and satisfy the faint."
Jeremiah 31:25

Lord,

I'm exhausted no matter the hours I lay on my pillow. The most small and mundane tasks demand all my energy to accomplish. It's a challenge to carry on conversations and stay on top of my schedule. Simply trying to get through the day feels like more than I can manage. It seems like a normal, productive life is slipping out of reach.

While it's difficult to give myself grace when I'm weak, I find loving compassion in You. You know I'm beaten down and You promise to build me up again. Today, I'm trusting and waiting on You to refresh my spirits. I believe when I'm overwhelmed and shutting down, You can quiet my panic and carry me through. Your love fills me up when nothing else brings peace or satisfaction. You are so good.

Amen.

72

Trust the Lord

Some trust in chariots and some in horses,
but we trust in the name of the LORD our God.
Psalm 20:7

Lord,

I need help. Yet who can I trust to provide what I need? Human advice falls short. Friends' and family's resources only go so far. My personal strength and determination grow weak and collapse. No self-help book, medication, or relationship will fully restore me in the end. Only You can heal me through and through.

Forgive me for doubting Your love and power. Lead me out of my struggle in Your perfect way and time. Show me the people, resources, and strategies You've prepared for my good. Teach me what it means to rest in Your promises to care for me. Loosen my grip so I release control and surrender to You. Reveal Yourself as my "mighty rock, my refuge" who I can trust to the end (Psalm 62:7).

Amen.

Known and Loved

For we do not have a high priest who is
unable to empathize with our weaknesses,
but we have one who has been tempted in
every way, just as we are—yet He did not sin.

Hebrews 4:15

Lord,

In this world, You suffered cruelty at the hands of evil men. You were abandoned by Your friends. Liars slandered Your precious name. You served the selfish and gave to the ungrateful. Your teachings and miracles were met with stubborn unbelief. You were not spared a single grief or pain this world can hold.

Because You suffered, You know what I'm going through today. Because You overcame You can help me to endure. Fill me with Your grace to forgive. Restore my hope that light will dawn in my life again. Show me You are here and that Your love won't let me go. Be my comfort and strength.

Amen.

74

A Spark of Joy

You, LORD, keep my lamp burning;
my God turns my darkness into light.
Psalm 18:28

Lord,

I've worn myself down from striving and struggling for far too long. I crave release from the pressure that never gives a moment's rest. In this state of burnout, it's hard to imagine how energy or optimism can ever be kindled again. I feel exhausted. Discouraged. Empty and cold. I need Your light to shine in my darkness today.

Let me know You as my "fountain of life" that refreshes, restores, and fills my soul (Psalm 36:9). Protect me from anything or anyone who works against me or my hope in You. Cleanse my mind from negative thoughts that deny Your promises to love and lead my way. Put strength into my weak body and spirit. Spark a joy-filled faith that cannot be extinguished by any forces of darkness around me.

Amen.

God Is Good

Even though the fig trees have no blossoms,
and there are no grapes on the vines...
yet I will rejoice in the LORD! I will be
joyful in the God of my salvation!
Habakkuk 3:17-18 NLT

Lord,

Even though my circumstances in this moment are not good, You are the good God You've always been. I struggle to see a way out of this darkness, but Your light of love shines on. I may suffer now but I'm holding on to faith that joy is found in You.

Open my eyes to see the ways You're giving me "daily bread" by meeting my needs and keeping me going (Luke 11:3). Let Your lavish love fill up my heart where hurtful relationships left me empty.

Fill me with gratitude for "so great a salvation" and the treasures that wait for me in eternity with You (Hebrews 2:3). You are my joy and my song in the night.

Amen.

Give your burdens
to the Lord,
and He will
take care of you.
He will not permit
the godly
to slip and fall.

Psalm 55:22 NLT

The One Who Heals

He heals the brokenhearted
and binds up their wounds.
Psalm 147:3

Lord,

The lack of love, support, and security I've suffered has left me with ugly labels written on my heart. Those labels say I'm alone. Unwanted. Shameful. Weak. Worthless. Undeserving. Hopeless. Tolerated at best and despised at worst. I grow afraid that I've been hurt and broken beyond repair.

Yet You, Lord, want to heal me with Your love. Your Word describes Jesus' own suffering that fills Him with compassion for mine. When others walk past me in my pain, You draw close. You speak tender words of grace to assure me I'm forgiven and I'm Yours. I'm promised strength to overcome my weakness and the enemies who come against me. In You, help and healing are found that will transform my heart, mind, and life. May I trust You for this until it is accomplished.

Amen.

77

Free to Forgive

"Do not seek revenge or bear a grudge against anyone among your people, but love your neighbor as yourself. I am the LORD."

Leviticus 19:18

Lord,

Hateful words have left me wounded and sore, crushing my sense of worth in the dust. Those who promised loyal love instead became a threat to my security and peace. I struggle to forgive the cold hearts who broke my trust. In my spirit, I crave justice for what I've been forced to endure.

Your Word says Jesus knows my pain. He bore abuse and rejection at the hands of those He came to love and save. By Your Spirit, put His humble heart of forgiveness into my own. Set me free from the heavy grudge I've strapped to my back. Heal my hurts. Erase all bitterness from my heart and mind so I can give the same grace You've given to me.

Amen.

A Gift of Praise

Through Jesus, therefore, let us continually offer to God a sacrifice of praise—the fruit of lips that openly profess His name.

Hebrews 13:15

Lord,

I don't feel joyful or glad in this painful season. My hope is wearing thin. I'm too tired to put on a brave face or figure out what to do. I feel I have nothing to offer You at all. So today, I simply give You my sacrifice of praise.

You, Lord, are where strength is found. The whole earth is full of Your glory (Isaiah 6:3). You have loved me with an everlasting love and drawn me close with unfailing kindness (Jeremiah 31:3). In Your infinite power, nothing is impossible for You. You are holy and perfect and Your Word is true. You are the Creator. Deliverer. Helper. You are all that is goodness and light. You are worthy of all love and praise.

Amen.

79

Change My Mind

The mind governed by the
flesh is death, but the mind governed
by the Spirit is life and peace.

Romans 8:6

Lord,

You know my story and the trauma I've experienced. You know the love I was denied and how others failed to meet my needs. And, You know how these sufferings ingrained beliefs in my mind that have kept me from living in freedom and truth.

I'm grateful for Your Spirit who can renew my mind and give me peace. Reveal the lies I've believed about my worth. Expose the blame and shame I've carried for the sins of others. Refresh my confidence in Your grace that cherishes me, forgives me, and delights to call me Your own. Let Your Word define my identity and purpose. Enable me "to grasp how wide and long and high and deep is the love of Christ" so I come alive in You (Ephesians 3:18).

Amen.

Secure in God's Love

If we confess our sins, He is faithful
and just and will forgive us our sins
and purify us from all unrighteousness.
1 John 1:9

Lord,

From the moment I put my trust in Jesus, You've been making me new. You forgive my sins and wash me clean. You brought me out of darkness into light. Though I've been hurt and abandoned by others, You cherish me as Your own. You promise to help me, keep me, and give me a "hope and a future" with You (Jeremiah 29:11).

Yet despite Your beautiful promises, I struggle to feel secure in Your love. Give me absolute faith in Your mercy so I'm free from doubt and shame. Fill me with confidence in my identity as Your child. Help me to face forward with the peace of a clean conscience. May I trust You with all my heart.

Amen.

Those who *live in the shelter* of the Most High will *find rest in the shadow* of the *Almighty*.

Psalm 91:1 NLT

All Is Possible

"'If you can'?" said Jesus.
"Everything is possible for one who believes."
Immediately the boy's father exclaimed,
"I do believe; help me overcome my unbelief!"
Mark 9:23-24

Lord,

Each day I live under this cloud of depression, it's more difficult to hold on to hope. Doubt creeps in as I wonder, *Will healing come? Has God forgotten me? Do I deserve what's happened? Am I too broken to put back together?* My belief is hanging by a thread as I wait for Your rescue. I can't sustain my faith on my own.

I pray that by Your Spirit, You will rekindle my hope and trust in Your love. Stir a joyful confidence in Your promises to save me and bless me with life to the full (John 10:10). Build up my strength so I can wait patiently for the goodness You have in store. All is possible with You.

Amen.

82

Your Cherished Child

But you are a chosen people, a royal priesthood,
a holy nation, God's special possession,
that you may declare the praises of Him who
called you out of darkness into His wonderful light.
1 Peter 2:9

Lord,

I thought by now I'd have overcome my challenges. Yet old wounds still sting. The loving relationships I long for have yet to flourish. Any achievements feel hollow. I don't feel strong or special. How can I take hold of my identity as Your beloved child?

Refresh my faith in Your Word that says I am cherished as Your "special possession" (v. 9). My life is not a random accident. You gifted me with a purpose in this world. I hold a place among Your chosen people both now and forever. The darkness cannot claim me since You called me into Your light. I am Yours, and I am loved.

Amen.

Side by Side

Brothers and sisters, we urge you to...
Encourage those who are timid. Take tender care
of those who are weak. Be patient with everyone.

1 Thessalonians 5:14 NLT

Lord,

Everyone seems busy with their own concerns. I know each person is carrying some kind of stress, hurt, or trouble. I wonder if it's fair to burden others with my problems. If I make myself vulnerable, will I be ridiculed or ignored? Will I be seen as weak or foolish? Should I be able to handle my hurts by myself? I need courage to ask for help and wisdom to know where help can be found.

Lead me to those who will meet me in the middle of this pain. Use them to encourage me when I feel like giving up. Provide godly guidance to navigate the road to a healthy mind and spirit. Cultivate grace-filled friendships that last. Let me know Your love through the love of others.

Amen.

84

The Good Shepherd

He tends His flock like a shepherd: He gathers the lambs in His arms and carries them close to His heart; He gently leads those that have young.

Isaiah 40:11

Lord,

I used to think that with determination, I could overcome any obstacle in my path. But now this battle with depression has brought me low. I'm tired of fighting. My spirit is wounded. My hopes have been disappointed again and again. I see how helpless I am to move forward on my own.

Thank You for inviting me to know You as my Shepherd. Show me how to draw close and surrender to Your care. Lead me toward healing, giving wisdom for each step to take. Feed me Your Word so it becomes "my joy and my heart's delight" (Jeremiah 15:16). Give me the heart of a lamb that trusts and depends on You for everything.

Amen.

My Confession

Therefore confess your sins to each other
and pray for each other so that you may be healed.
James 5:16

Lord,

I've left a wake of hurt behind me. At times I took more than I was willing to give in return. I've kept secrets, and I worked hard to hide the truth and preserve my image. I sinned in my anger by lashing out at those I love. When You reached out with compassion, I clung to my misery and rejected Your comfort. I've been selfish, proud, and unkind, and the wounds of my sin cut deep.

Give me the courage to confess my hurts and sins to those who will listen and care. Fill me with a humble spirit that is open to counsel. Lead me to those who will pray and walk the road of healing by my side. Use Your people to reveal Your mercy and love.

Amen.

"Be still, and know
that *I am God.*
I will be honored
by every nation.
I will be honored
throughout the world."

Psalm 46:10 NLT

My Help and Hope

Heal me, LORD, and I will be healed; save me and I will be saved, for You are the one I praise.

Jeremiah 17:14

Lord,

Each time I think depression is in the past, it brings me low once more. I wrestle again with fatigue, sadness, anger and shame. Life's sweetest gifts—the beauty of the seasons, time with loved ones, creative projects and plans—no longer delight my spirit. Will I ever celebrate a strength and joy that lasts?

I place my future in Your hands today. You can heal what's broken. You can renew my mind so I believe the truth of who I am as Your beloved child. Your power can save me from harm and redeem the pain of the past. In You, I will be made new. I praise You for Your goodness, love, and power to save. You give me hope!

Amen.

87

The Armor of God

Finally, be strong in the Lord and in
His mighty power. Put on the full armor
of God, so that you can take your
stand against the devil's schemes.

Ephesians 6:10-11

Lord,

Fatigue and depression leave me vulnerable to the enemy's lies. The devil tempts me to believe the future is hopeless. He shames me for my weakness. Determined to crush my faith in You, he tells me I'm worthless and unloved. Only Your power can save me from his destructive schemes.

Help me to stand firm on the truth of Your Word. Refresh my faith that by believing in Jesus, I am forgiven, saved, and Yours for all time. Nothing can separate me from Your love. You give me all I need to conquer sin and temptation. You are always working to take me to a place of healing, freedom, and peace. You are my strength and my light.

Amen.

Strength in Weakness

That is why, for Christ's sake,
I delight in weaknesses, in insults,
in hardships, in persecutions, in difficulties.
For when I am weak, then I am strong.
2 Corinthians 12:10

Lord,

If I'm honest, I can feel embarrassed that I struggle with depression. I compare myself to others who seem much more confident, positive, and brave than I am. Some have been critical or grown impatient with my slow healing. It's hard to admit I need support and compassion without feeling weak and small.

Yet You, Lord, create a new definition of strength. Strength isn't toughness—it's knowing how desperately I need You. It's only when I stop pretending I can make it on my own that I will fully know Your love and power. Use my heart wounds to show me Your goodness and build my faith. Be my strength as I put my trust in You.

Amen.

89

God's Good Work

I always pray with joy. . .being confident of this, that He who began a good work in you will carry it on to completion until the day of Christ Jesus.

Philippians 1:4, 6

Lord,

I yearn for laughter and lightness of heart. I dream of when I will face my fears with bold courage. My heart wounds long for comfort and healing. Yet for now, I feel trapped in a cycle of stress and sorrow with no end in sight. I'm clinging to Your promise to keep transforming my life day by day.

I pray for faith to believe Your love and power will save me. Convict me of any ways I've resisted You, disobeyed You, or shut You out. Open my eyes to see how You are working even now to bring me to peace and freedom. You will not leave me as You found me. There is great hope.

Amen.

Joy in Jesus

Those who look to Him for help
will be radiant with joy; no shadow
of shame will darken their faces.

Psalm 34:5 NLT

Lord,

The burden of depression holds a weight of guilt as well. I accuse myself with questions like, *Am I ungrateful for Your good gifts in my life? Is my faith too small? If I were a better, stronger person would I struggle this way? Am I a burden to those I love? Why can't I pull myself together? Are You angry or disappointed in me?* Overwhelming shame can stop me in my tracks.

I want to trust in Your merciful love. Help me to remember I'm saved through Jesus, adopted as Your child, and forgiven of all my failings. Silence the enemy's hateful accusations that tell me I'm unworthy and unloved. Remove the burden of guilt and "restore to me the joy of Your salvation" as I keep my eyes on You (Psalm 51:12).

Amen.

The LORD is my shepherd;
I have all that I need.
He lets me rest
in green meadows;
He leads me beside
peaceful streams.

Psalm 23:1-2 NLT

A True Friend

Like one who takes away a garment on
a cold day, or like vinegar poured on a wound,
is one who sings songs to a heavy heart.
Proverbs 25:20

Lord,

It can be easier to carry painful emotions in silence than to expose myself to cheery "encouragement" that leaves me worse off than before. My spirit longs for a listening ear that cares. I ache for someone to simply sit with me and honor my grief. The pressure to put on a smile and deny my heart's wounds only adds to the pain.

Thank You for Your merciful kindness as I heal. You never shame me, rush me, or ignore my cries. When I pray You always listen. When I feel discouraged and alone, You stay by my side. You know my needs in every detail. Because of Your love I know that joy is yet to come.

Amen.

92

In Need of God

"Blessed are the poor in spirit, for theirs is the kingdom of heaven. Blessed are those who mourn, for they will be comforted."

Matthew 5:3-4

Lord,

In my pride, I can pretend to have it all together. I can deny how helpless and broken I truly am. Instead of facing the reality of what's wrong in my heart and mind, I bury myself in distractions. Yet until I admit my need, I can't receive all the blessings, love, and healing You have in store.

I need You, Lord. I've believed so many lies that deny Your power, mercy, and love. Instead of following You as my Shepherd, I've let fear keep me stuck in my tracks. I've sought comfort outside of Your loving arms. Today I surrender to You. I believe You will forgive, heal, and bring blessing to my life. I am Yours and You are mine.

Amen.

God's Treasure

"Are not two sparrows sold for a penny?
Yet not one of them will fall to the ground
outside your Father's care…So don't be afraid;
you are worth more than many sparrows."

Matthew 10:29, 31

Lord,

So often I feel invisible to those around me. I keep my struggles to myself, even when the weight of pain seems too heavy to carry alone. My best efforts seem too small to make a difference to anyone. Cruel thoughts whisper that I'm worthless. Useless. Unwanted. I'm longing for comfort and love that lasts.

Thank You for Your Word that lights a spark of hope in my heart. You say I have value as Your chosen child. You promise to watch over me every moment. Your care is constant and I don't have to fear. By Your Spirit, fill me with faith to believe and courage to live like I'm loved.

Amen.

Firm in Faith

May the Lord direct your hearts into
God's love and Christ's perseverance.
2 Thessalonians 3:5

Lord,

You know how easily I slip into always-or-never thinking that says I'll never know happiness. I'll always give in to fear. I'll never find the help I need. I'll always fail, no matter how hard I try. I'll never experience a loving relationship where I feel cherished and secure. These lies crowd out the truth that I'm loved, I'm Yours, and You can do more than I ask or imagine.

Give me a tenacious faith that trusts You with all my heart. Sustain my hope that You are working for my good in every situation. Move me toward those who will love me like Jesus, and show me who I can bless in Your name. Let Your Scriptures's words of love saturate my heart so I believe You fully as my hope and Savior.

Amen.

Soften My Heart

Get rid of all bitterness, rage and anger, brawling and slander, along with every form of malice.
Ephesians 4:31-32

Lord,

I've been treated as if my needs don't matter. Impossible expectations have been held over my head. Others have hurt me and then blamed me for their actions. When I was most vulnerable, no one stood up to protect me. So much of life has felt cruel and unfair. How can I quench the fire of anger that burns inside?

I pray Your grace will help me to forgive. Guard my heart from bitterness that steals my peace and feeds a hateful spirit toward those around me. Help me to trust that You will bring justice in the right way and time. Bear Your fruit of patience in me so I'm slow to speak and slow to become angry (James 1:19). Fill me with the compassionate love of Jesus.

Amen.

Love never gives up,
never loses *faith*,
is always *hopeful*,
and *endures* through
every circumstance.

1 Corinthians 13:7 NLT

A Teachable Spirit

While he was still speaking, a bright cloud
covered them, and a voice from the
cloud said, "This is My Son, whom I love;
with Him I am well pleased. Listen to Him!"
Matthew 17:5

Lord,

Words are powerful. My memory replays how I was shamed and rejected. Accused and blamed. Deceived and misled. Others' words have sent me down destructive paths and denied Your wisdom, mercy, and love. It's only by listening to Your Word that I can know what's right and true.

Hide Your Word in my heart so instead of sinning, I think and speak and live by all You say (Psalm 119:11). Write over the lies I've believed with the truth of who You are and who I am as Your child. Use the Scriptures to teach me, change me, encourage and heal me as You make me new. Your Word is life.

Amen.

97

The Family of God

But pity anyone who falls and has no one to help them up. Also, if two lie down together, they will keep warm. But how can one keep warm alone?

Ecclesiastes 4:10-11

Lord,

It's a lonely world. Neighbors remain strangers. We hide behind screens instead of caring for one another face-to-face. Rather than sharing our burdens, we put up a brave front and carry the weight on our own. Yet this leaves us feeling broken, cold, and alone.

Thank You that out of Your love, You make a better way. I pray You will knit me into relationships where I can be supported and build others up, too. Show me how Your church can be like a true family. Place someone by my side who will accept me and challenge me at the same time. Draw me from this lonely place and into Your love.

Amen.

Guide My Steps

Surely you need guidance to wage war,
and victory is won through many advisers.
Proverbs 24:6

Lord,

In my battle for joy and peace, depression and anxiety are getting the upper hand. Where can relief be found? What is the cause of these difficult emotions? Do I need a doctor, therapist, prescription, or a self-help book to read? Is healing possible, or will I be bound by these struggles forever? My questions have no easy answers, and I don't know what to do.

Your wisdom is my hope. I pray You will provide trustworthy guidance to help me grow and heal. Show me who to listen to and whose counsel will take me in the wrong direction. Give me a humble, teachable heart that is willing to be challenged. Use others to bring me to a place of strength and maturity where I walk in freedom and joy.

Amen.

99

Courage in Christ

So we say with confidence, "The Lord is my helper; I will not be afraid. What can mere mortals do to me?"

Hebrews 13:6

Lord,

It's hard to know who to trust. Others have felt free to gossip and criticize behind my back. Those who claimed to care have stood me up and let me down. I've been bullied and blamed for weakness outside my control. The brave steps I've taken toward friendship have led me nowhere. I'm afraid to be vulnerable or open myself to anyone again.

Thank You that my heart is safe with You. You never fail to keep Your promises. You're gentle, honest, and kind. You listen each time I pray. As my Shepherd, You guide and protect me from harm. No matter how cruel this world might be, Your love goes on and on. Give me courage as I put my faith in You.

Amen.

My Comfort

I looked for sympathy, but there was none,
for comforters, but I found none.
Psalm 69:20

Lord,

While depression is a heavy burden to carry, it's even more difficult to bear it alone. Few have been willing to listen or try to understand. Others imply that I'm weak, foolish, or stuck in self-pity. I come away from conversations feeling shamed, as if I should be able to heal my own heart. Who will give me the comfort and support I'm longing to find?

Thank You that when I'm left alone in this world, You stay by my side. You hear my prayers and count my tears. Your Word tells me that Jesus, too, was "overwhelmed with sorrow" so He knows my pain (Matthew 26:38). You are kind and faithful, gentle and full of mercy as You keep me under Your wing. Your love is my comfort and peace.

Amen.

101

The Lord Who Listens

Turn to me and have mercy on me,
as You always do to those who love Your name.

Psalm 119:132

Lord,

The future is uncertain. I do not know when healing will come to my spirit. Relationships might reconcile or grow apart. My hopes may be fulfilled, or new dreams might take their place. Certain people may let me down while kindness and help arrive from unexpected places. I'm grateful that in this fragile and unpredictable life, You are faithful, loving, and true.

Thank You for the hope and security I find in Your love. You are the same yesterday, today, and forever (Hebrews 13:8). You speak the truth and keep Your promises. When I cry out to You, You always hear and respond. I don't have to fear You will abandon or reject me because Your love never fails. May I trust You all the days of my life.

Amen.

We don't look at the
troubles we can see now;
rather, we *fix our gaze*
on things that
cannot be seen.
For the things
we see now
will soon be gone,
but the things
we cannot see
will last forever.

2 Corinthians 4:18 NLT

About the Author

Joanna Teigen has been married to her husband, Rob, for over 30 years and celebrates life with their five children and grandchildren. As the co-founder of Growing Home Together, she believes their vows are for always, children are a gift, and prayer is powerful.

Joanna currently lives in West Michigan and is passionate to help people experience the power of God in their personal lives and family relationships.